MANNA

TRUSTING IN THE PROVISION OF GOD

WRITTEN BY ~ STEVEN LAKE

Manna – Trusting in the Provisions of God
Copyright © 2014 - 2024 by: Steven Lake
Written by: Steven Lake
Author Photo by: Steven Lake
Book Cover Design by: Donald Semora

ISBN Number: 978-1-940155-24-1

10 9 8 7 6 5 4 3 2 1

Published by: 2ᴖ 〔ᴴᴑᴣ 」ᴒᴪᴗᴛ〕 2ᴀ✦◯ 、ᴑᴅ

THE CHOICE IS YOURS.

RECEIVE CHRIST

THE WAGES
OF SIN IS
DEATH . . .

. . . BUT THE
GIFT OF GOD IS
ETERNAL LIFE.

A LIFE SEPARATED
FROM GOD
SIN
EMPTINESS
LACK OF PURPOSE
UNSURE OF ETERNAL
DESTINY

A LIFE IN HARMONY
WITH GOD
FORGIVENESS
ETERNAL LIFE
CHILD OF GOD
ABUNDANT LIFE
PEACE

MANNA
TRUSTING IN THE PROVISION OF GOD

The word "Manna" is a term that has come to mean many things to many people throughout the ages. But in its original Jewish context it meant "What is it?" This is because the Hebrew people didn't know what this strange gift from God was when they first saw it. But in the years and centuries since this simple word has taken on entirely new meanings, the most important of which is that Manna is a "special provision from God". Manna itself, at least in its original form, was a sticky, seed like substance similar to coriander in appearance with a texture not unlike gummy bears.

Numbers 11:7 (KJV) - *"And the manna was as coriander seed, and the colour thereof as the colour of bdellium."*

While the description of Manna may seem odd to some, it was God's way of feeding His people in the desert as they wandered for forty years to complete the punishment for their sin of unbelief at Canaan, and to change the people by getting Egypt out of their hearts. Even so, despite their sin, God provided them with food every day of their journey in the form of Manna so they would always have something to eat.

But this one special occurrence isn't the only time in history that God has done something like this for His children. He did it all throughout the bible and He's doing it even today, although we may not recognize it at times.

Philippians 4:19 (KJV) - *"But my God shall supply all your needs according to his riches in glory by Christ Jesus."*

Quite often, despite irrefutable evidence all around us that God will provide all of our needs (but not necessarily our wants), we fail to trust Him for His provision. In this book I hope to show you that not only can He be trusted for what you need, but also at *all* times and in *all* seasons. I also hope to show you how to recognize that provision in your daily life as it may not be all that obvious to you in the same way that it wasn't for myself for many years. Even today I'm still learning to recognize all of the provision God provides daily to myself and my family.

Points for Thought:
1. How and in what ways does God provide for you daily? List as many as you can.
2. What has been the greatest blessing or provision God has ever provided to you?
3. How much do you trust God for your provision?

My Personal Crisis Story

Sometimes it takes God hitting a person over the head before they'll pay attention or listen to Him. Jesus had to knock Paul to his knees on the Damascus road (Acts 9:1-19). God had to put Jonah in the belly of a whale (Jonah 1:17). Jacob (later renamed Israel) had to go through quite a few years of trials and a night wrestling with the per-incarnate Christ (Genesis 32:22-32) before God got his attention. And these aren't the only stories from the bible where God needed to take a "clue stick" to people before they finally got the message.

Even in this modern day it takes a lot to wake us up. Our world, our environment, and oftentimes our own selfish desires blind us to God's movement in our lives. But eventually He does reach us. It happened the day I got saved, and it's happened repeatedly throughout my life. If you can't tell I tend to be a bit thick headed about some things and sometimes only a good, solid crisis will awaken me to a truth. But once I've taken hold of that truth, I will not easily let it go. So there's some benefit to that stubbornness. It's from this platform that I present to you with one of the great crisis moments in my life which God used to get my attention.

It began late one night after a long day filled with worries. I'd spent most of that day, and the previous several, fretting over our food supply. While I can't say I've missed many meals, I was the kind of person who worried all the time about whether or not we had enough food on the shelves. This was especially true that night as our pantry was nearly empty and we had very little prospect of filling it anytime soon. This was primarily due to a series of events that'd drained our cash reserves dry, and left us with nothing to buy groceries with.

To give you an idea of how worried I was, my Mom told me later that she could see it in my eyes, hear it in my voice, and tell it in the way I was acting. While I wouldn't admit it at the time, I was scared. Maybe not to the level of terrified (Being ADD with Asperger's I would've emotionally shut down long before ever reaching that point), but enough that it was causing problems. I remember going to bed at my usual time around midnight and quickly drifting off to sleep. I figure the dreams kicked in about two hours later, and most were just random and wandering as usual, containing little of substance or significance.

However, sometime during those dreams I heard a panicked voice call out to me, like someone crying out in mortal fear. When I turned to see who it was I found myself surrounded by multiple dozens of people who were freaking out and running to and fro, while others wandered about looking like the walking dead. The latter group had bleach white skin, black lips, dark, hollow eyes, and a look of death on their face. I was immediately given the understanding that these were plague victims. I wasn't told what the plague was, but rather that it was spreading fast and killing a *lot* of people. Anyone who caught it was dying within hours without any hope of remedy or cure. Also, unlike the dreams I'd had earlier that night, this dream was hyper realistic. You could literally see, hear and feel everything as though you were wide awake and actually experiencing this for real. This wasn't the fuzzy fog of normal dreaming. This was one step short of reality. If you didn't know any better you'd actually think it was really happening.

Realizing I was in danger of becoming another victim of this plague I immediately ran for shelter in a large farm house just outside of town and rode out the worst of the plague there. When it finally ran its course I found myself living in a world almost completely devoid of people. To give you an idea of how bad the death toll was, in the dream I was told that only about 1% of the world's population survived the epidemic. Apparently those of us left alive were somehow immune to it, and thus weren't affected. Eventually I left the farm house and made my way into town. What I found was very grim and apocalyptic. There were piles upon piles of dead bodies lying everywhere in the streets, shops and vehicles scattered all around the village. In many ways it looked like Mad Max had paid a visit to the town and left his calling card.

Even more intriguing, there were no animals to be seen anywhere. Well, none alive anyways. Just death and plenty of it. The scene was very dark and bleak. Yet despite all this I didn't panic. I attribute some of that to both my Boy Scout and Army training. I was taught to remain calm and focused in the wake of an emergency, and do whatever was necessary to resolve the situation and survive. So for the most part I handled everything I encountered exactly as I'd been trained to do. Given that there was nobody around for miles in any direction, and likely wouldn't ever be, I immediately set about collecting supplies from the general area to ensure that I had ample food, medicine, water and anything else I'd need on hand. After all, it'd be rather pointless to survive the plague only to die of starvation or some other disease.

So I quickly got to work, and within a short time I'd amassed a nice sized stockpile of supplies that I could live off of for a year, maybe two if I took it easy. I was set. I was safe. I could weather this storm and come out the other side healthy, wealthy and free. But it was at this exact moment that God's voice came to me in the dream, and said, "It's good that you have this. But what will you do when the food runs out?" It was at that moment when sheer terror set in. To be honest, I didn't know what I'd do. I knew how to survive for the immediate future, just as I'd been trained to do, but what would I do five years down the line? Or ten?

How would I continue to live and survive once my horded supplies ran out? I really didn't know. That was because I knew deep down within myself that I didn't have the skills to survive for any great length of time without outside help or supply of modern resources. I'm by no means a "brown thumb" as some would call it. However, I have only a very basic understanding of gardening and farming, but none of the long term skills needed to survive past a year or two. For all intents and purposes, I was the walking dead. Despite having survived the plague, it wouldn't be long before I too would be dead.

So despite all I'd done, my chances of long term survival had dropped to zero. Shortly after this I awoke. But the fear of what I'd just seen didn't leave me. While I'd only been a dream, it'd brought to the forefront of my mind a truth I'd been denying or ignoring for many years. If everything I had and knew were taken away from me today, and I had no means by which to gain further subsistence of my own accord, I'd likely starve to death in less than a month.

That might seem a bit extreme, and highly unlikely in today's world, given the easy access to and wide availability of food, clothing, heat, cooling, and so many other creature comforts. But if you take all of those away, wipe everything off the map, and leave yourself with literally nothing but the cloths on your back, and no means to replenish your supplies, you'd quickly find yourself feeling much the same way I was at that moment. Realizing I had no means within myself to meet my own needs, I immediately dropped to my knees and cried out to God. I was sobbing like a little child, and the tears were rolling down my face in rivers.

For the first time in years I was genuinely afraid. I knew that, even though what I'd just experienced was simply a dream, it was still possible that something like that could happen for real. I didn't know how, but if massive, world ending disasters have happened before, and would absolutely happen again, what chance did I have? It was in the midst of this incredible, overwhelming tidal wave of fear that I heard one incredible, powerful word echo in my mind.

Manna

In that simple, one word statement I heard the answer to all my questions, to all my worries, to all my anxiety, to all my fear. Through that one word a peace that passes all understanding flooded over my soul. The fear that gripped me was washed away. In that one word a promise and an assurance was given to me that, no matter how bleak things become, how bare the shelves may get, how dark the day turns, God is always with me, and He will *always* provide my *every need*. It is His promise, in His word, from His very lips. To say it changed my life is an understatement. My mother could immediately see it in me the next morning when I got up. I had a skip in my step, a song on my lips and a smile on my face.

The fear was gone. In its place was an assurance and a truth that hadn't been there before. I'd read the Bible and knew the truths it contained about God's provision, but I'd never truly taken them to heart prior to that night. I'd always thought I was responsible for everything, not realizing that, while God holds us accountable to take care of a portion of our affairs (IE, we must both sow and reap), it is ultimately He who provides the bounty, the increase, the provision, and the supply.

Manna tells us that God *will* provide. Not might. Not maybe. He *will*. It is set in stone in His word. We merely have to trust Him for that provision. But is it a blind trust? Is there something we have to do, or is it entirely in God's hands? The answer is yes to both. But let me first explain myself so you better understand what I'm saying.

Point for Thought:
1. What personal crisis moment in your past brought you to an understanding of God's provision for your life?

JOSEPH

In Genesis 37-50, (and skipping chapter 38 as that's a side story about Judah) the story of Joseph is told. In this tidbit of biblical history God mightily shows His hand of provision in that, through Joseph, all in the known world at the time (or at least that region) were provided for, including Jacob and his family. The story begins with Joseph, the son of Jacob and Rachel, who was a dreamer at heart. Namely he was given the gift of dreams and the interpretation of them. The first recorded dream of Joseph was of the sheaves.

Gen 37:5-7 (NIV) - *"Joseph had a dream, and when he told it to his brothers, they hated him all the more. He said to them, 'Listen to this dream I had: We were binding sheaves of grain out in the field when suddenly my sheaf rose and stood upright, while your sheaves gathered around mine and bowed down to it.' "*

To those who don't understand the significance of prophetic dreams, they come in two forms. The first is a warning dream, such as was given to another Joseph, the father of Jesus.

Matthew 2:13 (KJV) - *"And when they were departed, behold, the angel of the Lord appeareth to Joseph in a dream, saying, Arise, and take the young child and his mother, and flee into Egypt, and be thou there until I bring thee word: for Herod will seek the young child to destroy him."*

They were warned in a dream to leave Bethlehem and flee to Egypt where the young Jesus would be safe. That is a warning dream. The second type is a prophetic dream. This details things in the future that *will* happen. If it predicts things that *may* happen and can be changed, then it is only a warning. If it is set in stone by God and is unchangeable, then it is prophetic. That is what Joseph's dream about the sheaves was. What makes this especially important is, if it's something that God says will happen, then it's a promise and since God always fulfills His promises, what is coming can't be changed or altered, as it is set in stone, as I mentioned before.

God does not change, nor does He waver from His promises. Ever. The problem we have with believing His promises is that we see people around us breaking their promises so often that it becomes hard to believe that God will keep His. Even so we should always trust God and His promises as they are sure, irrevocable, and always fulfilled. They just may not come together in the way we want or expect them to, or in a time and place that we'd like. However, they *will* be fulfilled.

A good example of this unfolds throughout the rest of Joseph's story. First he's sold into slavery (Gen 37:12-36), then he's faced with Potiphar's wife (Gen 39:1-23) who first tries to seduce him, and when that fails, she falsely accuses him, causing him to be thrown into jail for several years. Yet Joseph doesn't lose faith in God or His promises, even when it appears that the promises have failed again and again.

Genesis 39:2-6 (KJV) - *"And the LORD was with Joseph, and he was a prosperous man; and he was in the* *house of his master the Egyptian. And his master saw that the LORD was with him, and that the LORD made all that he did to prosper in his hand. And Joseph found grace in his sight, and he served him: and he made him overseer over his house, and all that he had he put into his hand. And it came to pass from the time that he had made him overseer in his house, and over all that he had, that the LORD blessed the Egyptian's house for Joseph's sake; and the blessing of the LORD was upon all that he had in the house, and in the field. And he left all that he had in Joseph's hand; and he knew not ought he had, save the bread which he did eat. And Joseph was a goodly person, and well favoured."*

Sure, Joseph was a slave, but within a very short period of time he ascends to the highest place within Potiphar's house, having full responsibility over everything in his house, save only for his wife. Everything else was handled by Joseph down to the last detail. But wait. Didn't Joseph get thrown into jail because of the false accusations of Potiphar's wife? Yes, but look what happened immediately afterwards.

Genesis 39:2-6 (KJV) - *"But the LORD was with Joseph, and shewed him mercy, and gave him favour in the sight of the keeper of the prison. And the keeper of the prison committed to Joseph's hand all the prisoners that were in the prison; and whatsoever they did there, he was the doer of it. The keeper of the prison looked not to any thing that was under his hand; because the LORD was with him, and that which he did, the LORD made it to prosper."*

That certainly doesn't sound like the promise failed yet, does it? Twice he's cast down, and twice God lifts him up and prospers him. To me it looks like the promise is very much alive and well. But that's not all. There's still another time when Joseph is riding high that he gets cast down.

Genesis 40 (KJV) - "*And it came to pass after these things, that the butler of the king of Egypt and his baker had offended their lord the king of Egypt. And Pharaoh was wroth against two of his officers, against the chief of the butlers, and against the chief of the bakers. And he put them in ward in the house of the captain of the guard, into the prison, the place where Joseph was bound. And the captain of the guard charged Joseph with them, and he served them: and they continued a season in ward. And they dreamed a dream both of them, each man his dream in one night, each man according to the interpretation of his dream, the butler and the baker of the king of Egypt, which were bound in the prison.*

And Joseph came in unto them in the morning, and looked upon them, and, behold, they were sad. And he asked Pharaoh's officers that were with him in the ward of his lord's house, saying, Wherefore look ye so sadly to day? And they said unto him, We have dreamed a dream, and there is no interpreter of it. And Joseph said unto them, Do not interpretations belong to God? tell me them, I pray you. And the chief butler told his dream to Joseph, and said to him, In my dream, behold, a vine was before me; And in the vine were three branches: and it was as though it budded, and her blossoms shot forth; and the clusters thereof brought forth ripe grapes:

And Pharaoh's cup was in my hand: and I took the grapes, and pressed them into Pharaoh's cup, and I gave the cup into Pharaoh's hand. And Joseph said unto him, This is the interpretation of it: The three branches are three days: Yet within three days shall Pharaoh lift up thine head, and restore thee unto thy place: and thou shalt deliver Pharaoh's cup into his hand, after the former manner when thou wast his butler. But think on me when it shall be well with thee, and shew kindness, I pray thee, unto me, and make mention of me unto Pharaoh, and bring me out of this house: For indeed I was stolen away out of the land of the Hebrews: and here also have I done nothing that they should put me into the dungeon.

When the chief baker saw that the interpretation was good, he said unto Joseph, I also was in my dream, and, behold, I had three white baskets on my head: And in the uppermost basket there was of all manner of bakemeats for Pharaoh; and the birds did eat them out of the basket upon my head. And Joseph answered and said, This is the interpretation thereof: The three baskets are three days: Yet within three days shall Pharaoh lift up thy head from off thee, and shall hang thee on a tree; and the birds shall eat thy flesh from off thee. And it came to pass the third day, which was Pharaoh's birthday, that he made a feast unto all his servants: and he lifted up the head of the chief butler and of the chief baker among his servants.

And he restored the chief butler unto his butlership again; and he gave the cup into Pharaoh's hand: But he hanged the chief baker: as Joseph had interpreted to them. Yet did not the chief butler remember Joseph, but forgot him."

Once again Joseph is knocked down, his chances at freedom dashed, with every indication that the promise has finally failed. But don't get discouraged just yet. If you've been paying attention you'll notice that Joseph has been knocked down three times, and raised up twice. Since God works in threes, there's still one more lifting up to come.

Genesis 41:8-44 (KJV) - "*And it came to pass in the morning that his spirit was troubled; and he sent and called for all the magicians of Egypt, and all the wise men thereof: and Pharaoh told them his dream; but there was none that could interpret them unto Pharaoh. Then spake the chief butler unto Pharaoh, saying, I do remember my faults this day: Pharaoh was wroth with his servants, and put me in ward in the captain of the guard's house, both me and the chief baker: And we dreamed a dream in one night, I and he; we dreamed each man according to the interpretation of his dream. And there was there with us a young man, an Hebrew, servant to the captain of the guard; and we told him, and he interpreted to us our dreams; to each man according to his dream he did interpret.*

And it came to pass, as he interpreted to us, so it was; me he restored unto mine office, and him he hanged. Then Pharaoh sent and called Joseph, and they brought him hastily out of the dungeon: and he shaved himself, and changed his raiment, and came in unto Pharaoh. And Pharaoh said unto Joseph, I have dreamed a dream, and there is none that can interpret it: and I have heard say of thee, that thou canst understand a dream to interpret it. And Joseph answered Pharaoh, saying, It is not in me: God shall give Pharaoh an answer of peace.

And Pharaoh said unto Joseph, In my dream, behold, I stood upon the bank of the river: And, behold, there came up out of the river seven kine, fatfleshed and well favoured; and they fed in a meadow: And, behold, seven other kine came up after them, poor and very ill favoured and leanfleshed, such as I never saw in all the land of Egypt for badness: And the lean and the ill favoured kine did eat up the first seven fat kine: And when they had eaten them up, it could not be known that they had eaten them; but they were still ill favoured, as at the beginning. So I awoke. And I saw in my dream, and, behold, seven ears came up in one stalk, full and good: And, behold, seven ears, withered, thin, and blasted with the east wind, sprung up after them: And the thin ears devoured the seven good ears: and I told this unto the magicians; but there was none that could declare it to me.

And Joseph said unto Pharaoh, The dream of Pharaoh is one: God hath shewed Pharaoh what he is about to do. The seven good kine are seven years; and the seven good ears are seven years: the dream is one. And the seven thin and ill favoured kine that came up after them are seven years; and the seven empty ears blasted with the east wind shall be seven years of famine. This is the thing which I have spoken unto Pharaoh: What God is about to do he sheweth unto Pharaoh. Behold, there come seven years of great plenty throughout all the land of Egypt: And there shall arise after them seven years of famine; and all the plenty shall be forgotten in the land of Egypt; and the famine shall consume the land; And the plenty shall not be known in the land by reason of that famine following; for it shall be very grievous.

And for that the dream was doubled unto Pharaoh twice; it is because the thing is established by God, and God will shortly bring it to pass. Now therefore let Pharaoh look out a man discreet and wise, and set him over the land of Egypt. Let Pharaoh do this, and let him appoint officers over the land, and take up the fifth part of the land of Egypt in the seven plenteous years. And let them gather all the food of those good years that come, and lay up corn under the hand of Pharaoh, and let them keep food in the cities. And that food shall be for store to the land against the seven years of famine, which shall be in the land of Egypt; that the land perish not *through the famine. And the thing was good in the eyes of Pharaoh, and in the eyes of all his servants.*

And Pharaoh said unto his servants, Can we find such a one as this is, a man in whom the Spirit of God is? And Pharaoh said unto Joseph, Forasmuch as God hath shewed thee all this, there is none so discreet and wise as thou art: Thou shalt be over my house, and according unto thy word shall all my people be ruled: only in the throne will I be greater than thou. And Pharaoh said unto Joseph, See, I have set thee over all the land of Egypt.

And Pharaoh took off his ring from his hand, and put it upon Joseph's hand, and arrayed him in vestures of fine linen, and put a gold chain about his neck; And he made him to ride in the second chariot which he had; and they cried before him, Bow the knee: and he made him ruler over all the land of Egypt. And Pharaoh said unto Joseph, I am Pharaoh, and without thee shall no man lift up his hand or foot in all the land of Egypt."

Three times struck down. Three times lifted up. The best part of this is that in the end Joseph is lifted up to a position of authority second only to Pharaoh, and even higher than Potiphar who'd been his master for a time. During the next seven years Joseph set about putting away grain for the years of famine that God predicted. Remember the prophetic vs warning dreams I told you about earlier? Here's a biblical example of a prophetic dream. Through the following years of famine God used Joseph and the grains they'd set aside to make Egypt the most powerful nation in the world, and to force his family to come to Egypt, and to ultimately reunite Joseph with his family.

At the end of the day God's promise, as laid out in the dream, was fulfilled. But not just His, but also the dreams of the two servants and Pharaoh's as well! So God didn't just fulfill one promise. He fulfilled FOUR! So how's that for a track record? Four for four. But those aren't the only examples of God fulfilling His promises. There's many more! Read on to see some other great examples of God's provision and Manna.

Points for Thought:
1. Name three promises God has made to you and ultimately fulfilled in your life.
2. Identify at least three other promises God has made in the bible and ultimately fulfilled.
3. Search the scriptures and list every promise God has made and fulfilled.
4. List all the promises God has yet to fulfill.

NOAH

Hebrews 11:7 (KJV) - *"By faith Noah, being warned of God of things not seen as yet, moved with fear, prepared an ark to the saving of his house; by the which he condemned the world, and became heir of the righteousness which is by faith."*

One of the more famous stories of faith in the Bible, which is ultimately trust in its purest form, is that of Noah. From the time of Adam to the time of Noah mankind multiplied across the Earth and as they did, great evil and wickedness followed with them. So much so that God considered wiping out everyone in a massive flood and starting over again. But he found Noah and his family to be righteous in His sight, so He promised to spare them even though He'd still wipe out the rest of the planet. Noah in turn believed God's promise and set about building an ark for the saving of his family as he'd been told to do. But what makes this especially interesting is how God provided for him.

God gave Noah a complete blueprint of the boat, sent the animals, provided plenty of resources to build the boat, and even three sons to help him build it! There's also another proof that Noah believed God's promise of the flood. Up to that time it'd never rained on the planet, yet he never questioned God, nor stopped building the Ark, or preaching righteousness to an unbelieving world even though it took him a hundred years to do it. He believed God so much that he kept right on doing what he'd been commanded to do, despite the persecution, mockery and the fact that there hadn't been a single drop of rain in the entire history of the world up to that point.

Genesis 2:6 (KJV) - "*But there went up a mist from the earth, and watered the whole face of the ground.*"

Even though it'd never rained on the Earth even one day up to that point, Noah still believed what God told him and acted accordingly. But now you might ask, "I thought God was providing everything for Noah? So why did he have to do all that work and labor a hundred years to build the ark? If God provided all his needs, why didn't He also build the Ark for Noah?" As I said, God will provide all our needs. But He also commands us to do our part as well.

Genesis 3:19a (NIV) - "*By the sweat of your brow you will eat your food...*"

By the sweat of your brow. That certainly sounds like work, doesn't it? You will eat your food. That in turn is God's provision. You work as God has directed, and He will provide. There are times that the provision is miraculous, and sometimes it's mundane. But either way you're still required to do your part. Look at the Hebrews and the Manna in the desert. God provided, but they had to go out and gather it every day as God told them to. It wasn't set before them, or just placed in their hands. God provided, but they had to gather. Or what about animals? God provides for them, but they still have to go out and get it.

God expected no less of Noah. He was given everything he needed to build the Ark, including all of the raw supplies, and then ordered to make it happen. And ya know what? Noah obeyed. It's one of the reasons you're here today reading this. If he hadn't obeyed, you wouldn't be alive today. Let alone born. So consider that the next time you choose to disobey God. Your seemingly insignificant actions can have massive ramifications for the future.

Proverbs 10:4 (NIV) - *"Lazy hands make for poverty, but diligent hands bring wealth."*

2 Thessalonians 3:10 (KJV) - *"For even when we were with you, this we commanded you, that if any would not work, neither should he eat."*

So if you work, and you ask for God's provision, He will supply your every need at exactly the right time and in the right way, but not a minute before its needed, nor a minute after. And it will always be in the right amount, the right type, and in the right place, no more, no less, no further. Just like God did with Noah.

Genesis 5:32 (KJV) - *"After Noah was 500 years old, he became the father of Shem, Ham and Japheth."*

Genesis 6:22 (KJV) - *"Noah did everything just as God commanded him."*

God said it. Noah did it. That right there is a perfect example of faith and trust in God's provision; the essence of Manna. Now as you suspect God brought the flood just as

He'd promised and saved Noah and his family, and all those aboard the ark, just as He'd promised. So does that mean we can trust God for the little things in our lives, as well as the big ones? I think that's a resounding yes. But how does trusting God for our provision, our "Manna" if you will, apply in today's world? The answer might surprise you.

But before we get to that, I have a feeling that some of you still need more proof that God does meet every one of our needs. So let's look at a few more ancient and modern day examples of God's provision and the fulfilling of His promises given throughout the ages.

Points for Thought:

1. How can you apply the faith of Noah in your own life in trusting God for His provision?
2. What obstacles are there in your life to trusting in God's provision?
3. What can you do to remove those obstacles?

ISRAEL

There were many, many promises in the Bible given to Abraham, Issac, and ultimately Jacob, who later became Israel. The most well-known of these is the promise of the number of descendants that Israel would have. God has always fulfilled His promises throughout history. However, they haven't always been fulfilled in the lifetime of the person they were given to, as in the case of the patriarchs. God once promised to Abraham that he would have a son, and it would be a special child, born of Sarah, his wife. But God didn't fulfill that promise right away. He instead waited until Abraham was very old and well on in years, long past the age at which either he, or Sarah, could have children. Yet God did eventually fulfill his promise through the birth of Issac, despite Abraham's brief failure to believe that culminated in the birth of Ishmael.

Genesis 16:1-4 (KJV) - *"Now Sarai Abram's wife bare him no children: and she had an handmaid, an Egyptian, whose name was Hagar. And Sarai said unto Abram, Behold now, the LORD hath restrained me from bearing: I pray thee, go in unto my maid; it may be that I may obtain children by her. And Abram hearkened to the voice of Sarai. And Sarai Abram's wife took Hagar her maid the Egyptian, after Abram had dwelt ten years in the land of Canaan, and gave her to her husband Abram to be his wife. And he went in unto Hagar, and she conceived: and when she saw that she had conceived, her mistress was despised in her eyes."*

God waited as long as He did to ensure that He alone would get the credit for this miraculous birth. However, Abraham's failure to believe and trust in God's promise resulted in a child that eventually became the father of the Arab people who have ultimately been a thorn in the side of the Israelites throughout all of history. Just like trusting and believing in God's provision has great benefits, failing to do so in turn has great consequences, as is aptly demonstrated. But trusting God's provision has far more rewards than simply a fulfilled promise or a met need in your life. Sometimes just the act of waiting builds patience, which in itself is a blessing (even though some may disagree). Take one of Daniel's prophesies as an example.

Daniel 9:24-27 (KJV) - *"Seventy weeks are determined upon thy people and upon thy holy city, to finish the transgression, and to make an end of sins, and to make reconciliation for iniquity, and to bring in everlasting righteousness, and to seal up the vision and prophecy, and to anoint the most Holy. Know therefore and understand, that from the going forth of the commandment to restore and to build Jerusalem unto the Messiah the Prince shall be seven weeks, and threescore and two weeks: the street shall be built again, and the wall, even in troublous times.*

And after threescore and two weeks shall Messiah be cut off, but not for himself: and the people of the prince that shall come shall destroy the city and the sanctuary; and the end thereof shall be with a flood, and unto the end of the war desolations are determined. And he shall confirm the covenant with many for one week: and in the midst of the week he shall cause the sacrifice and the oblation to cease, and for the overspreading of abominations he shall make it desolate, even until the consummation, and that determined shall be poured upon the desolate."

To date the entire prophesy has not yet been fulfilled. But here's the exciting part. Most of it has. The first part of this prophesy was fulfilled when the decree was given to rebuild Jerusalem and its walls by Cyrus, the king of Babylon, in 445BC. The second part of this prophesy was fulfilled on the day that Jesus made His triumphal entry into Jerusalem. The last week of years however has yet to be fulfilled. So while not all of this promise has been completed, most of it has, yet again proving God's faithfulness.

Ezekiel 37:12 (KJV) - *"Therefore prophesy and say unto them, Thus saith the Lord GOD; Behold, O my people, I will open your graves, and cause you to come up out of your graves, and bring you into the land of Israel."*

Isaiah 11:11-12 (KJV) - *"And it shall come to pass in that day, that the Lord shall set his hand again the second time to recover the remnant of his people, which shall be left, from Assyria, and from Egypt, and from Pathros, and from Cush, and from Elam, and from Shinar, and from Hamath, and from the islands of the sea. And he shall set up an ensign for the nations, and shall assemble the outcasts of Israel, and gather together the dispersed of Judah from the four corners of the earth."*

Another thing God promised was to bring Israel back into their land someday, and in 1948 He did just that. But if you notice the verse says that this would be done a "second time". This is because there was two regatherings. The first was out of Persia after the fall of Babylon. The second was out of the nations (ie, the world) which happened in 1948. God promised both regatherings, and both times He delivered. For the first one we only have the bible and a scattering of historical records to go by. For the second however we have not only recorded modern history and documentation that we can look at (videos, youtube, movies, tv, etc), read about (internet, books, newspapers), and hear about (audio recordings), but there are also eye witnesses who still remember and can testify to the day when it happened and can tell you where they were, and even what they were doing. But the fulfilling of these promises, and the making of provision for Israel (restoring the land to them), is only the tip of the iceberg. God has done much, much more.

One of the most visible of these provisions has been repeated safety for Israel. In 1948, immediately after the nation was reborn, all of her Arab neighbors declared war on her and flooded across the borders in an effort to wipe out the Jews and drive them into the sea. But time and time again during that war God blessed Israel and gave her victory over her enemies, ultimately securing her freedom, sovereignty, and right to exist as a nation. Then in 1967 the six day war occurred, and in less than one week it was over with Israel once again the victor. In 1973 came the Yom Kippur war, a surprise attack by the Arab nations on Israel during her highest holy day that lasted a total of 20 days, after which Israel was again victorious.

And these are only the big wars. There are numerous small ones as well. Even so, every single war that Israel has been in, it's won. Or has it? No, Israel itself didn't win them. *God won those wars.* Israel merely did the work and God gave the provision. In this case it was a provision of safety and victory. Even so God provided their needs just as He said He would. He even blessed the land and made barren, unfruitful, worthless desert bloom. The fruit and produce that is produced in Israel is second to none in the world. God has even recently given them oil to provide wealth and resources during a time when they're increasingly being cut off from outside sources of funding.

He's blessed the nation with increasing prosperity through education, science, medicine, and more. Some of the greatest breakthroughs in the world are coming out of Israel, many of which you wouldn't expect, including advancements in the fields of physics, chemistry, optics, medicine, economics, biochemistry, and much more. But it's not just modern Israel that's been blessed. Remember the wilderness wanderings? God provided for Israel during that time. We all know about the Manna God sent to feed them. But there is another, lesser known, yet still highly important provision that Israel received during that time.

Exodus 17:6b (KJV) - *"Strike the rock, and water will come out of it for the people to drink." So Moses did this in the sight of the elders of Israel."*

That's right. God provided them water from a rock. Later on, during the time that Jesus walked the Earth, God provided food, shelter, and all manner of needs for the seventy that Jesus sent out on a brief missionary journey, as well as the twelve disciples who were the first to go out.

Luke 10: 4 (KJV) - *"Carry neither purse, nor scrip, nor shoes: and salute no man by the way."*

Jesus sent them on their way to do His work with nothing more than the cloths on their back and the staffs in their hands. Yet every one of their needs were met on that trip, and when they returned they had some incredible stories of provision that they shared with Christ and others. Then of course there was the feeding of the five thousand.

Matthew 14:13-21 (KJV) - *"When Jesus heard of it, he departed thence by ship into a desert place apart: and when the people had heard thereof, they followed him on foot out of the cities. And Jesus went forth, and saw a great multitude, and was moved with compassion toward them, and he healed their sick. And when it was evening, his disciples came to him, saying, This is a desert place, and the time is now past; send the multitude away, that they may go into the villages, and buy themselves victuals. But Jesus said unto them, They need not depart; give ye them to eat. And they say unto him, We have here but five loaves, and two fishes.*

He said, Bring them hither to me. And he commanded the multitude to sit down on the grass, and took the five loaves, and the two fishes, and looking up to heaven, he blessed, and brake, and gave the loaves to his disciples, and the disciples to the multitude. And they did all eat, and were filled: and they took up of the fragments that remained twelve baskets full. And they that had eaten were about five thousand men, beside women and children."

And the four thousand as well which came later.

Mark 8:1-9 (KJV) - *"In those days the multitude being very great, and having nothing to eat, Jesus called his disciples unto him, and saith unto them, I have compassion on the multitude, because they have now been with me three days, and have nothing to eat: And if I send them away fasting to their own houses, they will faint by the way: for divers of them came from far.*

And his disciples answered him, From whence can a man satisfy these men with bread here in the wilderness? And he asked them, How many loaves have ye? And they said, Seven. And he commanded the people to sit down on the ground: and he took the seven loaves, and gave thanks, and brake, and gave to his disciples to set before them; and they did set them before the people.

And they had a few small fishes: and he blessed, and commanded to set them also before them.
8 So they did eat, and were filled: and they took up of the broken meat that was left seven baskets. And they that had eaten were about four thousand: and he sent them away."

But that isn't all Jesus did. He healed the sick, raised the dead, cast out demons and so much more. As you can see, this is just a tiny scratch on the surface of what God the Father did for Israel through Himself, through Christ, and through the

Holy Spirit. God has repeatedly provided for Israel's needs, and is still doing the same today in so many incredible ways.

Points For Thought

1. How many times has God miraculously provided for Israel as a nation?
2. Name some of the forms that provision took.
3. Name the people God used to bring about some of those provisions.

RUTH

If you read the entire book of Ruth you will discover that Ruth is the daughter-in-law of Naomi, a Jewess. While Ruth is the main character here, Naomi is the one to whom the promise is given. But what promise is that?

Leviticus 25:25 (KJV) - *"If thy brother be waxen poor, and hath sold away some of his possession, and if any of his kin come to redeem it, then shall he redeem that which his brother sold."*

While this verse might seem a little vague, it speaks volumes not just for the Jewish people, but even for us. If you follow the rest of the chapter from verse 25 onward it gives a list of things you need to do in a variety of situations for the promise to be fulfilled. To the western mind this verse likely doesn't make sense. So to understand it properly you have to first know that in ancient Israel land was not bought and sold the way we think of it with permanent ownership changing hands. Over there the original family who took claim to it during Israel's initial settling was the same family who would own it forever. Land would only fall into the ownership of another family if no kin claimed it, either due to disinterest in reclaiming it for a relative, or the death of the family line that owned it.

So if you sold your land to someone else who wasn't a family member or direct kin, it was theirs only for a select period of time before it automatically returned to you at the time of Jubilee. So when the land was "sold", it was actually rented for a specified period of time rather than outright owned by the purchaser. This was, for all intents and purposes, a promise of provision from God. Let me explain a little further so you understand why and this begins to make more sense. In ancient Israel land was everything. It was wealth, a means of subsistence, and a way by which to gain income. Without it, your prospects of financial security were pretty slim. God knew that and made sure that it was hard to lose your land.

In order for your land to be lost in those days you really had to go completely out of your way to do it. So if you were forced to sell it in order to pay off some debts, or even feed your family, God provided you a way to get it back at some point. That's where the story of Ruth comes in. According to the Bible, Naomi and her husband were forced to sell their land due to a crushing drought that'd swept over the land and impoverished everyone. Shortly after this they packed up their things and left for Moab where they planned to stay until the drought ended.

While there Naomi's two sons took Moabite wives, and then both of them, plus her husband, died. In bitterness and sorrow she sent both her daughter-in-laws away, but Ruth stayed behind while the other left and returned to her family. After this Naomi and Ruth left for Israel. But because of the famine, and later the death of the husbands, they were now dirt poor. So upon arriving they set about harvesting grain in the corners of the fields, which was made available for all the poor to keep for themselves as prescribed in the Torah and the law. It was God's method of provision for anyone who was impoverished or in need, but unable to earn a living.

Along the way Ruth meets Boaz (a relative of Naomi), falls in love, and eventually marries him. After this Boaz redeems the lands that were once owned by Naomi and her husband, and through this the law of the kinsman redeemer was fulfilled and God brought wealth and happiness to both women. But that's not the best part. In the process of meeting Ruth and Naomi's needs, He puts in place another important element of biblical history involving the then as yet coming Messiah. Take a look at this verse from the book of Matthew and you'll see what I mean.

Matthew 1:5 (KJV) - *"Salmon begot **Boaz** by Rahab, **Boaz** begot **Obed by Ruth**, **Obed** begot **Jesse**, and **Jesse** begot **David the king**."* (emphasis mine)

As we all know, Jesus was born from the line of David. But along the way God used a Moabitess as part of His plan of salvation. Why? What did God gain by including a gentile woman in the Jewish genealogy of Christ? I think it was a foreshadowing of the day when God, through Christ, would graft the gentile nations into His plan of salvation.

Romans 11:24 (KJV) - *"For if thou wert cut out of the olive tree which is wild by nature, and wert graffed contrary to nature into a good olive tree: how much more shall these, which be the natural branches, be graffed into their own olive tree?"*

Acts 1:8 (KJV) - *"But ye shall receive power, after that the Holy Ghost is come upon you: and ye shall be witnesses unto me both in Jerusalem, and in all Judaea, and in Samaria, and unto the uttermost part of the earth."*

"The uttermost parts of the world." That certainly sounds like us gentiles, doesn't it? So God used Ruth, a gentile, to make possible the birth of Obed, then Jesse, and eventually David, while leaving a message in the genealogy for us to find centuries later, telling the whole world that they're just as important in the plan of salvation as the Jews are. I'm certain He could've done it without Ruth, yet He chose to include her as a sign that we too would one day be brought into God's kingdom and saved through our kinsman redeemer, Jesus Christ. If that's true then this is a clear case of God fulfilling promises within promises, and using His provision of their needs as a means to move forward His grand plan for history. Is that cool or what?

Point for Thought:
1. How has God been a kinsmen redeemer in your life, bringing back to you things you've lost?

ESTHER

The book of Esther is another great example of God providing for a need in someone's life. In the case of Esther that provision was for the entire nation of Israel and the saving of the Jewish people. To properly understand the story you first need a bit of background. The problems that Esther was dealing with started way back before King David was put on the throne.

1 Samuel 15:3 (NIV) - *"Now go, attack the Amalekites and totally destroy all that belongs to them. Do not spare them; put to death men and women, children and infants, cattle and sheep, camels and donkeys."*

The two people in question in this verse are King Saul (the one receiving the order), and Samuel the prophet (the one relaying the order from God). By all accounts this seems like a normal command of God as He was quite regularly sending Israel out on various wars and excursions to bring judgment to evil countries and tribes, so this was nothing out of the ordinary. Where this becomes a problem is when Saul fails to follow the orders given to him.

1 Samuel 15:7-9 (NIV) - *"Then Saul attacked the Amalekites all the way from Havilah to Shur, near the eastern border of Egypt. He took Agag king of the Amalekites alive, and all his people he totally destroyed with the sword. But*

Saul and the army spared Agag and the best of the sheep and cattle, the fat calves and lambs—everything that was good. These they were unwilling to destroy completely, but everything that was despised and weak they totally destroyed."

God told Saul, through Samuel, that he was to destroy *everything*. Not just the people, nor the cattle, nor certain things. Everything. Period. So when he (Saul) got done, he was to leave *nothing* alive, at all, under any circumstances. If it drew breath, from the king all the way down to the tiniest baby calf, it was to be slain. That was his orders from God. But instead Saul took a spoil of the Amalekites from their herds and flocks, which he was told *not* to do, and kept it for himself and his men. He also allowed Agag the king to live, as well as one of his offspring. That offspring in turn gave rise to the Agagite tribe, from which Haman, the chief villain in the story, descended. So Saul's sin then became Israel's problem years later, and if historians are to be believed (because it doesn't say it in the bible), that particular sin is still causing problems even today in the form of Jew and Christian hating, blood thirsty terrorist organizations such as Hamas, Hezbollah and others.

So just as Adam's sin cursed the entire human race, Saul's sin cursed all of Israel throughout history up to this present day. It's into this world that Esther steps. At the beginning of the book God uses the Persian king Xerxes (the same one made famous by the battle of Thermopylae) to bring Esther, a Jewess, into power as queen of Persia. This was the first step God took in providing for a major need in the lives of the exiled Jews even though they didn't know it. As the story progresses Haman appears within the narrative and quickly cheats his way to the top. Part of this is because he lusts for power and control, and partly because he wants to bring about the annihilation of the Jews as part of a long standing hatred and desire for revenge that has been brewing within his people for centuries.

This hatred predates the Agagites and goes all the way back to the Amalekites, who hated the Jewish people first, even all the way back to the days of the Exodus, and sought to kill them every chance they got. It's from this background of hatred that Haman comes. And it doesn't take long for him, after gaining power, to seek the destruction of the Jewish people. He does this by deceiving the king into condoning and facilitating his genocidal plan. (Note: Xerxes is another name for Ahasuerus, the first of three Persian kings to take the title Xerxes.)

Esther 3:8-11 (KJV) - *"And Haman said unto king Ahasuerus, There is a certain people scattered abroad and dispersed among the people in all the provinces of thy kingdom; and their laws are diverse from all people; neither keep they the king's laws: therefore it is not for the king's profit to suffer them. If it please the king, let it be written that they may be destroyed: and I will pay ten thousand talents of silver to the hands of those that have the charge of the business, to bring it into the king's treasuries.*

And the king took his ring from his hand, and gave it unto Haman the son of Hammedatha the Agagite, the Jews' enemy. And the king said unto Haman, The silver is given to thee, the people also, to do with them as it seemeth good to thee."

At this point, for all intents and purposes, the Jews were doomed. But if Haman had succeeded in seeing his plan fulfilled, God's promises to the Jewish people would've been broken, both of their protection, and their future destiny. So God provided a way out right in their greatest moment of need, at the right place, the right time, and in the right way.

Esther 4:13-14 (KJV) - *"Then Mordecai commanded to answer Esther, Think not with thyself that thou shalt escape in the king's house, more than all the Jews. For if thou altogether holdest thy peace at this time, then shall there enlargement and deliverance arise to the Jews from another place; but thou and thy father's house shall be destroyed: and who knoweth whether thou art come to the kingdom for such a time as this?"*

Yes, Esther was that way out, that provision in their time of need. God knew their need *before* they asked for it or even knew they had one, and had already put in place the means by which to fulfill it long before Haman became a problem.

Esther 8 (KJV) - *"So the king and Haman came to banquet with Esther the queen. And the king said again unto Esther on the second day at the banquet of wine, What is thy petition, queen Esther? and it shall be granted thee: and what is thy request? and it shall be performed, even to the half of the kingdom. Then Esther the queen answered and said, If I have found favour in thy sight, O king, and if it please the king, let my life be given me at my petition, and my people at my request: For we are sold, I and my people, to be destroyed, to be slain, and to perish. But if we had been sold for bondmen* *and bondwomen, I had held my tongue, although the enemy could not countervail the king's damage. Then the king Ahasuerus answered and said unto Esther the queen, Who is he, and where is he, that durst presume in his heart to do so?And Esther said, The adversary and enemy is this wicked Haman. Then Haman was afraid before the king and the queen.*

And the king arising from the banquet of wine in his wrath went into the palace garden: and Haman stood up to make request for his life to Esther the queen; for he saw that there was evil determined against him by the king. Then the king returned out of the palace garden into the place of the banquet of wine; and Haman was fallen upon the bed whereon Esther was. Then said the king, Will he force the queen also before me in the house? As the word went out of king's mouth, they covered Haman's face. And Harbonah, one of the chamberlains, said before the king, Behold also, the gallows fifty cubits high, which Haman had made for Mordecai, who spoken good for the king, standeth in the house of Haman. Then the king said, Hang him thereon. So they hanged Haman on the gallows that he had prepared for Mordecai. Then was the king's wrath pacified."

Haman meant to kill all the Jews by subterfuge and trickery. But God used Esther to foil his plan and save the Jewish people. So throughout all of this God not only knew their needs, he provided the means to fulfill them *before* they knew they had any, and in a way much *greater* than they'd requested. How so? Well, not only did God save them from death, he also allowed them to destroy their enemies and take a spoil for themselves.

Esther 8:11 (KJV) - "*Wherein the king granted the Jews which were in every city to gather themselves together, and to stand for their life, to destroy, to slay and to cause to perish, all the power of the people and province that would assault them, both little ones and women, and to take the spoil of them for a prey,*"

Now, if God can do that for Israel, to not only save them from destruction, but bless them and increase their wealth and possessions as a result, how hard is it to believe that God can provide *all* your needs *all* the time, anytime, anywhere, anyhow, no matter what?

Jehovah Jireh

The name "Jehovah Jireh" means "God My Provider" or "God Provides". Provision is one of God's names. But there are also many others names that God holds dear. Here's a few examples. Jehovah Rapha, "The Lord Who Heals". Jehovah Nissi, "God our banner of love and protection." Jehovah Shalom, "Our Perfect Peace". Jehovah Shammah, "The Lord is with us everywhere, for he is omnipotent." Jehovah Sabbaoth, "The Lord of Hosts (ie, armies), our Protector." El Shaddai, "The Lord God Almighty." These are only a few of the many, many names of God, and each one describes a different attribute of His. Peace, healing, love, protection, omnipotence, and so much more. If each of these is a characteristic of God himself, and ultimately the trinity (Father, Son, Holy Spirit), how difficult is it to believe that God can provide <u>ALL</u> your needs down to the very last detail?

Philippians 4:19 (KJV) - *"But my God shall supply <u>all</u> your needs according to his riches in glory by Christ Jesus."* (emphasis mine)

God can provide every one if your needs, because God owns everything. Yes, everything. You, your cloths, the trees around your house, your car, your very life. God owns it *all.* We are just stewards of the things we possess in this world. They are God's exclusive property and His alone. He created them, and they are His, but we are given charge or stewardship of them for a brief time to use for *His* honor and *His* glory, and not our own. So if He owns it all, how hard is it to believe that He can provide our needs no matter where we are?

To me it's not hard at all. But I suspect that some of you still don't believe that, nor do you believe that God owns everything. So I will provide you with another example that I hope will drive this fact home to you. God created the universe. He created all light, all matter, everything. He created you, and me, and every other thing. He even created the very atoms and elements we are made of down to the very tiniest string of energy. But one thing He's never done with anything in this universe at any point in history is transfer ownership from Himself to anyone else. Never. It has remained His exclusive property from time immemorial, and will remain that way forever. God even told Adam and Eve they were "stewards" of the garden. Not owners. Stewards.

The only reason we believe we "own" anything is because our culture tells us we can. This is derived from generations of men and women who believed that if they owned something they controlled it, and thus the more they owned, the greater control they would have over the things in this world, and ultimately greater power. But there is *nothing* in this universe which God has transferred ownership away from Himself and to anyone else. That includes you. It was His, still is, and always will be. He's never sold it to anyone, nor given it as a gift. The only exception to this rule is the gift of salvation that He has given to all. However, salvation is not ours until we accept it. Until then it remains as God's property. Even so, that's the only thing we can wholly, physically and completely own ourselves and nothing else. Therefore we are not, nor ever will be owners of anything in this world. We are merely stewards of what we've been given of which we'll be required to give an account of when we stand before God someday.

1 Timothy 6:6-7 (KJV) - *"But godliness with contentment is great gain. For we brought nothing into this world, and it is certain we can carry nothing out."*

When you die, what can you take with you? Nothing. Not a house, a car, a boat, or even a grain of sand. The only thing you can take with you to Heaven is your salvation, and absolutely nothing more. So when you die your soul departs for either Heaven or Hell and all you "own" here in this world, including your body, is left behind. If you truly owned it, wouldn't you be allowed to keep it? Yes, you would. But since you're merely a steward of it, when your work here is done you must leave it all behind. Except salvation. Again, that is the *only* thing you can ever own and the *only* thing you can take with you after death. That you can take with you to Heaven, but that and only that. Nothing else.

So if God is our creator and our master, and we are merely His stewards within this world that He created which is entirely His and under His complete ownership, how difficult is it to believe that God can give us what we need? He already owns it all, so for Him to give us everything we require to meet our daily needs requires absolutely no effort on His part whatsoever. So if we ask God in faith (while God can and will provide your needs, you must also believe that He is able to do so) to provide our needs, He will be gracious and give to us what we ask for or require.

But we must understand that anytime we ask for something we need to remember that our needs are more than just food, shelter or finances. There are other needs, such as protection, knowledge, wisdom, greater faith, courage, and so much more that are just as important. Also, your needs don't necessarily have to be physical in nature. They can be spiritual as well. In fact, the vast majority of your needs *are* spiritual. So at times the fulfilling of your physical needs in turn supplies a spiritual need in your life at the same time. Hence why they are so readily granted. But what if the denial of your physical needs fulfills a greater spiritual need? Yes, it is entirely possible that a times, being denied a physical need actually meets a spiritual need.

That might not make sense, but if you look at the bigger picture it does. You are not flesh. You are a spirit. It's sort of like what CS Lewis once said. "You aren't a soul with a body. You *are* a soul. You *have* a body." Why do you think it says in the bible that on the day of the rapture that we will be given *new bodies*? If we're giving new bodies, doesn't that mean that it's the soul that's the real us, and the most important part at that? It also means these fleshly bags of dust and water are merely temporary housing until the day when the Lord gives us new, eternal, sinless, flawless, immortal bodies that never get sick or die.

2 Corinthians 5 (KJV) - *"For we know that if our earthly house of this tabernacle were dissolved, we have a building of God, an house not made with hands, eternal in the heavens."*

1 Corinthians 6:19 (KJV) - *"What? know ye not that your body is the temple of the Holy Ghost which is in you, which ye have of God, and ye are not your own?"*

Our bodies are an earthly house. A temple if you will; a place in which our spirit dwells and takes up residence. That's why our provision is sometimes spiritual and sometimes physical. But ultimately, even when the need being fulfilled is physical, it is meant to supply our spiritual needs first of all and above all. So always remember that God *will always* provide. But sometimes we have to do our part to make good on that blessing. For example, God may bless you with a car, but you have to buy it. God may provide you with food, but you have to accept it. In a sense that's very much like how salvation works. Christ came to Earth, died on a cruel cross and shed His blood for the remission of our sins, was buried and on the third day rose again, forever taking captive death and Hell, and paying for all of our sins in their entirety.

In this simple act God provided for our need of salvation from our many sins, which is arguably the greatest need we will ever have, bar none, and He did it before we ever knew we needed it. However, while you don't have to "earn" your salvation, thanks to Christ's once and for all payment for sin through His death on the cross, there is still one thing you must do to make it our own. Christ's sacrifice was a _gift_, and as such, in order for the gift to become yours, you must accept it. This is true of any gift. It *does not* become yours until you accept it.

Remember what I said earlier. Salvation is of God, and thus it is His to give to any He should choose to. Just because God owns everything doesn't mean He can't give it to us to own for ourselves if He so chooses. And if we accept His gift of salvation it will become ours and stay with us forever. And it will be the one and only thing we will ever be allowed to own in all of eternity. Sure, Christ had to come to this world to make it possible, but it's a gift none the less, and it's the only thing He gives to us that we can truly own. I just can't say that enough times.

But to become the recipient and owner of this gift, you *must* accept it. Until you do, the gift sits in God's open hands for you to look at and to study, but remains entirely His until you accept it and take it as your own. Here's another way to look at it. Let's say I have a dollar bill and I offer it to you as a gift. Even though I've offered it to you, that dollar is still mine and will remain mine until you physically take it from my hand and make it your own. Salvation is the same way. As a gift you must truly, fully and completely accept it and take it as your own before it can become yours.

Points for Thought:
1. List all of the names of God. (use a concordance for this if you must)
2. List all of the meanings for those names.
3. How do these names define God? What attributes of God do they identify?
4. What do these names mean to your life?
5. Find at least two ways each of these names can be applied to your walk with God.

BEING GOD'S HAND OF PROVISION TO OTHERS

Psalm 41:1-2 (KJV) – "*Blessed is he that considereth the poor; the Lord will deliver him in time of trouble. The Lord will preserve him, and keep him alive; and he shall be blessed upon the earth; and thou will not deliver him unto the will of his enemies.*"

Proverbs 19:17 (KJV) – "*He that hath pity upon the poor lendeth unto the Lord; and that which he hath given will he pay him again.*"

Have you ever considered the thought that part of the reason why God blesses you and provides for your needs is so you can in turn bless and provide for others?

2 Corinthians 9:7 (KJV) - "*Every man according as he purposeth in his heart, [so let him give]; not grudgingly, or of necessity: for God loveth a cheerful giver.*"

God takes all of the gifts that you give and uses them for a wide variety of purposes within His Church body. This includes everything from paying the salaries of church employees to spreading the gospel around the world, or even helping those who are less fortunate in your community.

Numbers 18:21 (KJV) - "*And, behold, I have given the children of Levi all the tenth in Israel for an inheritance, for their service which they serve, [even] the service of the tabernacle of the congregation.*"

Another interesting fact, which most may not know, is that up until the last century or so, and for most of history at that, it was believers, both in the Old Testament (BC) and the New Testament (AD) periods that God used to provide the needs of others. In antiquity there was no such thing as welfare or public assistance, save for a handful of brief, sporadic cases throughout history, such as the Roman empire. For the most part though the only charity or welfare that people saw in their lives was provided by those who believed in and trusted in God. In some cases that was provided completely free of charge to those in need through an act of charity by one of God's people. But in most cases it was gained through work, such as the gleaning of leftovers after the harvesters had cleared the fields. In other words, people worked for their "public assistance".

Leviticus 19:9-10 (KJV) - "*And when ye reap the harvest of your land, thou shalt not wholly reap the corners of thy field, neither shalt thou gather the gleanings of thy harvest. And thou shalt not glean thy vineyard, neither shalt thou gather every grape of thy vineyard; thou shalt leave them for the poor and stranger: I am the LORD your God.*"

To help those in need God even provided a welfare system of sorts in the Law of Moses that went above and beyond normal charitable giving that people did. However, that system was dependent on the actions of the individual. Sure, you could get free food, but you had to earn it by going out and actually gleaning it from the fields, or harvesting it from the vines. But in the end most all of the charity you received was from those who obeyed God's law.

Malachi 3:8-10 (KJV) - *"Will a man rob God? Yet ye have robbed me. But ye say, Wherein have we robbed thee? In tithes and offerings."*

We must always remember that God owns everything, right down to the very last atom within our bodies. I just can't drive home that point enough. We are only stewards, and **_NOT_** owners. As such, it should not come as a shock when God asks us to give a portion of what we have to help someone else, as it already belongs to Him to begin with and is therefore His to do with as He chooses. It would be like me handing you my coat for safe keeping, and then asking you to give it to someone else who is cold. It's the same basic idea. It's still my coat, but you're the steward who has been entrusted briefly with it's care and then later told to give it to another person who needs it more. Giving to others as God commands is essentially the same thing.

So if God asks you to give an offering to the church, or even to an individual, don't do it grudgingly, but gladly with joy, because in doing so you will demonstrate to God and others that you are not only a good steward of what God has given you, but also worthy of yet greater gifts. So the more you surrender to God, and the more willingly and cheerfully you give as God asks, the more He will in turn give you until your cup is overflowing like a raging river.

Points for Thought:
1.	What ways in my life can I be a blessing to others?
2.	What things in my life has God asked me to give to others, be it money, things, or even my time?
3.	What things do I have at my disposal that I can do or give more of to God's service?
4.	Do I give cheerfully to God and others, or do I give grudgingly.
5.	How can I show the love of God to others through my giving?
6.	Is my giving selfish, or selfless?
7.	Is my giving for my own honor and glory, or for God's?

GOD'S WILL (NEEDS)
VS
OUR DESIRES (WANTS)

Oftentimes in this world we get our needs and wants confused. Needs, by definition, are things you can't live without. Wants, in turn, are things you desire or would like to have, but they're not required for your survival or to allow you to continue operating and living your life. Even so, far too often we ignore our real needs and instead strive for the things which do not edify us, or worse yet, unnecessarily or harmfully clutter up our lives. These can be simple things, or they can be big things. It's one of the key points I use when teaching others how to live frugal. I ask them, "What do you really need?" What they say in reply is often quite revealing, and almost immediately tells me where their heart really is.

One of the better stories I've heard from people in regards to this comes from a friend who was ministering to a poor family in the area. The man he was helping almost couldn't put food on the table, was in jeopardy of being kicked out for not paying his rent, and many other things. Yet when they went into his house, my friend was stunned to see this man and his family had a 52" plasma TV, an Xbox, a Nintendo Wii, a Sony PlayStation, a DVD player, a Blue Ray player, a Roku, iPhones, iPads and half a dozen other electronic gadgets and things. When asked about this, the man said, "But I've gotta have my entertainment!" My jaw nearly hit the floor when I heard that. Here you have a man who clearly had the means to put food on the table for his family, and yet his "entertainment" was more important to him that eating!? That is likely the most perfect example I've seen so far of crossed priorities. But don't go and wag your head just yet. We're just as guilty of the same thing, although maybe not in the same extreme degree.

As you have clearly seen, this man's needs were being superseded by his wants. But there's a bigger issue here than merely getting needs and wants confused. His problems weren't a head issue caused by failed logic. It was completely and entirely a heart issue. Allow me to explain. The issue of mixed up needs and wants is similar to the problems I see when witnessing to people. When I walk them through the plan of salvation and they say yes, oftentimes they only make a mental assent to the Lord, but fail to make a true decision or commitment in their heart. IE, they agree to salvation mentally, but their hearts never change. In some ways it's similar to what Christ said about the Pharisees and their lip service.

Matthew 15:8 (NIV) - *"These people honor me with their lips, but their hearts are far from me."*

Matthew 23:27 (KJV) - *"Woe unto you, scribes and Pharisees, hypocrites! for ye are like unto whited sepulchres, which indeed appear beautiful outward, but are within full of dead men's bones, and of all uncleanness."*

As I said before, the failure to properly discern true needs vs wants is a heart problem, not a head problem. Some of that is due to our society, and some due to natural sinfulness. We are so instinctively and naturally drawn to sin that to let go of those sinful desires and surrender entirely to God's will and provision is hard. It's like what one theologian once said, "They missed it by 18 inches," pointing to the relatively short distance between one's head and one's heart. "These people honor me with their lips (head), but their *hearts* are far from me." In other words, they agreed to the gospel logically, but it failed to make the 18 inch journey from their heads to their hearts. The same is true with wants vs needs. We acknowledge our wants with our heads, but fail to make the 18 inch journey to our hearts to confirm what are our true needs.

That thought alone ought to say a lot about why we don't properly discern between what are our real needs and those things which are only selfish, sometimes sinful wants. Now, going back to the guy who clearly had his priorities mixed up, let's examine that a bit further and break it down, using the logic I just presented. Where did his problems truly lie? Was it that he didn't have enough money? Clearly that's not the case given the thousands of dollars' worth of stuff he had. Even if he paid on credit he still had to pay the credit card bill each month, and that would've been exorbitant given what he owned. So money wasn't the issue. And although I didn't mention it, his shelves were filled with video games, movies, and the like. So again, money wasn't the issue. Then why was he so worried about having his entertainment? For the observant person the answer is simple.

He needed Christ. He was trying to fill a God shaped hole in his heart, as some refer to it, by filling it with the things of this world. But as has been proven many, many times before, trying to do that is a vain, hopeless effort. It may provide you with a temporary distraction, but it's never truly fulfilling, which makes you want more and more of it. You fill the void with worldly things, which don't fill the void, so you get *more* worldly things to fill the void, which they still fail to do, and on and on it goes in a vicious, never ending circle. It's why people on drugs can't get enough and become addicted. In the same way needless things can become an addiction. It never satisfies you and ultimately leaves you back where you started wanting something else, something greater to fulfill your needs. The only thing that can completely, totally, and absolutely satisfy all of your needs is a relationship with Jesus Christ, and that can only be had through accepting His gift of salvation that He bought for you with His blood on the cross of Calvary.

But what if he'd been a believer? What if this was a Christian doing this? Would he be subject to the same problems as the unbeliever? Well, yes and no. Yes in the fact that we're still human, so we all are vulnerable to the same temptations. However, with a Christian we have Jesus we can run to. The unbeliever has nothing. Even so we can still foolishly fill our lives with junk that takes us away from our relationship with Christ. Trust me, this is something the Devil loves to do, because the weaker your relationship with Christ, the less you're able to hinder his work. So if you are truly, honestly, fully believing, trusting, and living for Christ, your priorities will almost always align with the will of God and in turn your eyes will be opened to see what things are truly needs in your life, and what things are just unnecessary clutter.

Another way to look at our needs vs our wants is through the lens of idolatry. Remember that God shaped hole we have in our hearts? Not the fleshy hearts in our chests that pump blood. I'm talking about your living soul. While the expression is only figurative, it does detail a very clear and definitive truth. Without God we are empty. With God we are full. But how much God fills us depends on our relationship with Him. It's why we sometimes fill our lives with needless things. If Christ isn't filling every crack and crevice of who we are, we will instinctively turn to the world in search of other inferior, often sinful things to fill that painful gap in our lives.

For a good example of how bad this frivolous filling can become, I take you to an example I posted about in my blog not long back. But before I begin, I believe you need a little background first. For those who don't know me, I'm an auction hound. I love auctions and the "thrill of the chase" that comes with it. I rarely buy much while I'm at them as I don't need much. Even so I enjoy simply being there, watching the bidding wars, the people as they battle with each other over various items, the way they duel with each other, and how the sale goes down. To me it's fascinating to watch and a lot of fun to be a part of. Well, anyhow, as the year was unfolding around me, an auction came up on my radar that piqued my interest. It was a living estate sale (ie, the guy was still alive, but they were selling off his possessions by court order) for an elderly gentleman up in Olivet, MI. But this wasn't a normal sale or a normal guy. This gentleman completely and fully fit the description of a hoarder to a T.

He had barns and barns and barns full of stuff, hard side car shelters, houses, cars, etc all packed to the gills with things. (No, I'm not joking. He really did!) I don't think this guy threw anything away. Ever. Period. It was like he'd buy something, use it a few times, then toss it aside. Some things were even brand new and never used, and in many, many multiples of the same thing. Every single building on his property was stacked to the roof. It took **_nine_** auctions to get rid of all his stuff. _Nine_ of them. And those weren't just little sales. We're talking sales with an average of two auction rings (and sometimes more) that each ran for _at least_ seven hours each sale day just to get rid of the stuff. For anyone who knows auctions, a typical sale lasts between two to four hours, with three hours being the most common duration. So for one of them to last seven hours and only touch a tenth of what this guy had says a lot given how fast stuff moved at these auctions. And yes, my math seems a bit off. Nine auctions that each only moved a tenth of what he had. So where's the other tenth?

That was hauled away in dumpsters. Not "dumpster". _Dumpsters_. Plural. We're talking the big ten cubic yard jobs you'd see at construction sites. I think there was at least four to five of those taken out, that I know of at least, and that was only a tenth of what he had. Yes, a tenth. That by itself should give you a fuller perspective of just how much he had. Now in retrospect, this was a gentleman who clearly had a needs complex. He was trying his level best to fill that God shaped hole with every single thing he could get his hands on. I'd be willing to wager that it didn't work given how much he had accumulated. But are we any better? Let's go back to the example at the beginning of this section. Do we really need

TV's to begin with, especially given the garbage on the airwaves these days? Do we really need our expensive phones or media players, or even our iPods?

The answer is a clear and definitive no. If we can't live without them then we're clearly not living our lives right. Many would argue to the counter, but I disagree. Yes, they're nice to have, but they're not a need. At the end of the day we can live without them. But when it comes to God, He's the one and only thing in our lives we can't live without. And yet we seem content to file Him to the far end of our priority list rather than at the very beginning. So if putting God first in our lives is truly difficult for us, what can we do to correct that? Well, the answer is simple. If *anything*, and I mean *anything*, puts itself BEFORE God in *any way* in our lives, it's an idol and needs to be disposed of, destroyed, sold off, or otherwise gotten rid of.

That includes *ALL* things we put before God priority wise in our lives. We may not bow down and worship them as the pagans once did, but we might as well as what we're doing is the same thing. So if there's something in our lives that gets between us and God, and does so consistently, then it needs to be gotten rid of. But what about food, or clothing, or shelter? Aren't those needs, and don't they hold a high priority in our lives? They do. But then the next question is, where do they stand in regards to your relationship with Christ?

Matthew 6:31-33 (NIV) - "*So do not worry, saying, 'What shall we eat?' or 'What shall we drink?' or 'What shall we wear?' For the pagans run after all these things, and your heavenly Father knows that you need them. But seek first his* *kingdom and his righteousness, and all these things will be given to you as well."*

We need to seek God *first* in all things! Then, when we do, He will supply for you anything else you need. There is the key to needs vs wants. You *need* God. You *want* things. And God *provides* needs. The world *offers* wants. So keep the right priority of things in your life and God will see to it that you have everything you *need*. Remember, everything in this life is about God and should always be about God. So the next time you go to get something, or you pick up something you already have and use often, first stop and ask yourself, "Does having this bring honor and glory to God?" That might seem like an odd question to ask yourself. But remember this: It's *not* about you. It never was. Everything in this world, including everything you do is and must be for *God's Honor* and *His Glory*, and not your own. Period. He must be first, and we must be last. That's why the things we see as needs are not the same things that God sees as needs, and since we are His creation made for His glory, we should always keep that simple thought in mind.

Isaiah 55:8-9 (KJV) - *"For my thoughts are not your thoughts, neither are your ways my ways, saith the LORD. For as the heavens are higher than the earth, so are my ways higher than your ways, and my thoughts than your thoughts."*

Remember, God is much bigger than we are, He knows more than we do, and He's seen more than we have. Therefore, God in turn knows our needs far better than we could ever hope to, and our primary need is Him and Him alone. That doesn't mean we can't have other things. It simply means that we must be circumspect and take a very close look at every so called need in our life and determine if it is truly a need, or merely a selfish desire that does not edify, or more importantly, separates us from God or hinders our relationship with Him. Therefore we must ask ourselves, what things are there in our lives that God knows are our greatest needs? If you're not certain, then I recommend using the JOY principle to help you determine the value of something.

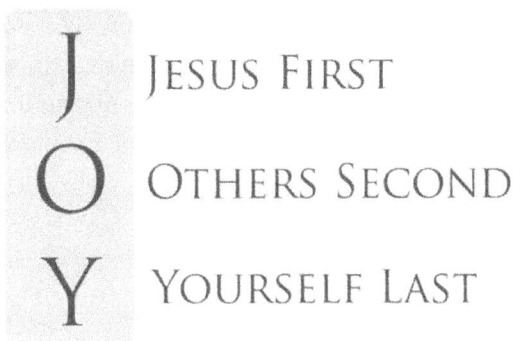

J JESUS FIRST

O OTHERS SECOND

Y YOURSELF LAST

The principle states simply, put Jesus first in your life, others second, and yourself last, and you will find true joy. You will also discover through this experience the things which are your true needs. For example, when using it to determine a need vs. a want, ask yourself, does this item bring honor and glory to Jesus, or God? Does it bless and edify others? Or is this strictly for my honor and glory, or selfish desires? If you do this it will help you correct your way of thinking, and your view of the world. It will also help transform your life in ways you could never imagine.

Points for Thought:

1. Look for ways in your daily life to serve God and Christ. What things to they ask you to do, or what things can you do to serve them daily?
2. In what ways do you put Christ first in your life?
3. What things can you do to put Christ even more in charge of your life?
4. What ways can you work to put others before yourself in your daily life?
5. Write out a list and identify all of your needs and wants as you see them. Now take that list and pray about it and let Christ show you where your thinking is wrong, and where it's right, then ask Him to reshuffle the list into its correct priority.

STORMS AND GOD'S PROVISION

One of the biggest social phenomenon's of the 21st century has been what is most commonly referred to as the "prepper" movement. These are people who carefully and thoughtfully set aside food, water and resources for what they perceive to be a coming "doomsday", be that the end of the world, a pole shift, hurricanes, tornadoes, or something as simple as the loss of a job. Some people might say, "Oh they're just a bunch of crazy tin foil hatters." But are they? Is the "prepper" movement nothing but a modern day fad perpetrated by "doomsaying" lunatics, or is there something more? Could it be possible that they're actually very wise in doing something that God has demanded of everyone? Well, as always, let's look and see what the bible says about that.

Proverbs 6:6-8 (NIV) - "*Go to the ant, you sluggard; consider its ways and be wise! It has no commander, no overseer or ruler, yet it stores its provisions in summer and gathers its food at harvest.*"

Proverbs 30:25 (NIV) - "*Ants are creatures of little strength, yet they store up their food in the summer;*"

Hebrews 11:7 (KJV) - "*By faith Noah, being warned of God of things not seen as yet, moved with fear, prepared an ark to the saving of his house; by the which he condemned the* *world, and became heir of the righteousness which is by faith."*

Genesis 41:34-36 (NIV) - *"Let Pharaoh appoint commissioners over the land to take a fifth of the harvest of Egypt during the seven years of abundance. They should collect all the food of these good years that are coming and store up the grain under the authority of Pharaoh, to be kept in the cities for food. This food should be held in reserve for the country, to be used during the seven years of famine that will come upon Egypt, so that the country may not be ruined by the famine."*

Throughout the Bible God has repeatedly told his people to set back provision for the future, even if the skies are clear, and there's not a cloud in sight. He did it with Noah, and Joseph, and countless others. However today, anyone who puts back more than a few days' worth of food is seen as a fanatic and a "doomsdayer". Yet all through history putting back a store of supplies for "the winter" or "hard times" was the normal thing to do. For our ancestors it wasn't "prepping". To them it was just good common sense, as you were seen as a fool if you *didn't* put away at least something for the winter (which, by all definitions, is an annually occurring natural disaster, believe it or not) or hard times ahead. This was especially important since most items they gathered and ate were seasonal and only available for a brief period of time each year.

So for most, putting away a stockpile of supplies was how you did things. You harvested your food in the fall, and ate off that supply all year long until the next harvest came in. So is putting away food and other supplies anti-biblical, or as one author recently called it "anti-faith"? Is saving up for the future trials and hardships of life, especially in a modern world full of abundance, considered as circumventing the provision of God? Absolutely not, and let me show you why! Let's begin by looking at the January 17th, 1994 Northridge, California earthquake. Those who'd gone out of their way to set aside food and water well in advance for just such a situation were warm, well fed, and even able to help others through the tragedy that'd cut off all water and power to the city at one of the worst times of the year! (Yes, even California gets cold in January) Those who didn't were cold, starving, and miserable for months afterwards.

Or what about Hurricane Sandy that hit the east coast in 2012? Or Issac that same year? Or Katrina in 2005? Those who'd made appropriate preparations in advance had all they needed to get through the disaster and help others who were in need. Notice a pattern here? If we're following God's will, then we should always prepare for that day of trouble that *will* come into our lives. It's not an *if*, but a *when* as history has proven time and time again. So we should work as the ant does and put away supplies for that rainy day that will come at some point. It's never an *if*, but always a *when*. We should always prepare for that day of uncertainty as God has directed, and in turn warn others of what's coming so they too can prepare. As I mentioned before, both Noah and Joseph did it. One prepared an ark for the saving of his family and all living creatures of the Earth, and the other prepared a nation (Egypt) for a coming famine.

So simple preparation, however you want to call it, is not only biblical, but is a commandment from God. If you're willing to listen to His command to prepare now, and always be prepared, He'll give you the information and resources you need in the good days so you can put away supplies for the lean days that *will* come. In doing so, God provides for us *before* the storm, because once it comes there is no more time to prepare, nor gather. So all that remains for you now is to decide how much to prepare, and for what kind of events. But that is something which is between you and God alone to determine. Nobody else can decide that for you except God Himself. But once you know, once God has made it clear to you what you must do, work quickly, diligently, and wisely.

The point is, you don't know what is coming, but God does. He also knows how much and exactly what you will need to get you and your family through whatever disaster you will face. For some He may say you only need 3 days of food and water. For another, two weeks. For another 3 months, and so on. He might tell one that they need a boat. For another it may be a cow, or something as simple as a camp ax. Don't automatically assume you need to store 50 tons of food or 20 years' worth of supplies. That's just stupid, and for all intents and purposes it's wasteful hording because most of that stuff will go bad before you ever use it. But as I said, discuss this at length with God and find out what He wants you to put away for that coming "rainy day". If you listen, He'll guide you in everything you must prepare in preparation for those leaner times.

And those leaner times might not be on a local, state or national level. They may exist only in your home. Say your house burns down, or you lose your job. Isn't that a disaster in itself? And before you think that any of this is crazy, ask yourself this. Do you buy car insurance? What about home or renter's insurance? Do you have health coverage? A savings account? Contrary to popular belief, all of those things are each a different means of preparation for an uncertain future. So putting away something for hard times, be it food and water, tools, fuel, etc to prepare for an as yet unforeseen disaster that is somewhere out on the horizon is not crazy.

God demands that we do it, so as believers we must obey. Besides, you already do it anyways, so how is this any different than what you're doing now? The only difference really is that with insurance, or even a savings account, your putting your safety through the storm into the hands of others. That is fine for the lesser disasters of life. But for the bigger ones, the only one you can rely on is God, and His provision. So if you're prepared in the way God has directed you, then you can be assured safe shelter in the storm. It may not be easy, and it may get rough along the way, but it's better than the alternative. So be obedient like Noah and Joseph. Prepare for the storms that will come, and then trust in God's provision through the storms when they do come.

FUTURE TRUST

Trusting in God's provision isn't just for today, or tomorrow, or next week. It's for from now through eternity. There is a day coming when Christ will return in the clouds, with a shout, and a trumpet, and the voice of the archangel to bring His elect home.

1 Thessalonians 4:16-17 (KJV) - "*For the Lord himself shall descend from heaven with a shout, with the voice of the archangel, and with the trump of God: and the dead in Christ shall rise first: Then we which are alive and remain shall be caught up together with them in the clouds, to meet the Lord in the air: and so shall we ever be with the Lord.*"

There are many things coming, including future Manna that God will give to us who are His called out ones, His children, His saints. But you must believe in Jesus Christ, that He died and rose again, and paid the penalty for *your* sins, and you must place your entire trust in Him for your salvation. God brings rain upon the just and the unjust, to edify and bless the saved, and to reach out and win the lost. He doesn't wish that any should perish, but that all should have eternal life.

Proverbs 30:4-5 (NIV) - "*Who has gone up to heaven and come down? Whose hands have gathered up the wind? Who has wrapped up the waters in a cloak? Who has established all the ends of the earth? What is his name, and* *what is the name of his son? Surely you know! "Every word of God is flawless; he is a shield to those who take refuge in him."*

God is all powerful, all knowing, and all seeing. He knows our needs, and He is able to provide all of those needs. All we need to do is be obedient and trust Him.

Hebrews 11:1 (KJV) - *"Now faith is the substance of things hoped for, the evidence of things not seen."*

So put your faith in Christ, prepare for the future, one that is guaranteed to be uncertain, and trust Him every day for your provision. He *will* provide. All you need to do is have faith that He will. Even in your darkest hour, trust the Lord always.

GOD'S BLESSING OF SALVATION

By now you already know that God can and will supply all of your needs be they physical or spiritual. But above everything your spiritual needs are most important, and the most important of these is salvation; your reconciliation to God and the eternal forgiveness of all your sins. But how is this possible? How does one get saved? The answer is simple. However, let me begin by covering the basics, and the biggest of these is to acknowledge that you're a sinner.

Romans 3:23 (KJV) - *"for all have sinned and fallen short of the glory of God."*

Second, you must understand that the wages of sin is death. Yes, death. Banishment forever in Hell separated from God and everyone you love and everything you love. Total isolated, tormented separation forever. The ultimate solitary confinement.

Romans 6:23 (KJV) - *"For the wages of sin is death, but the gift of God is eternal life through Christ Jesus our Lord."*

But do not despair, for there is hope. Even before we knew we were sinners, lost and without God, He sent His only Son Jesus to die for everyone, even you, long, long before you were ever born. Yes, He knew you so well He knew you'd sin even before you were born, and He cared enough for you that He sent Jesus to die in your place, and Jesus also loved you so much that when sent He gladly went, knowing beforehand the incredible pain and suffering He would have to endure on your behalf. That is true love, far above anything that exists in this world, and is the truest love of all.

Romans 5:8 (KJV) - *"But God demonstrates his own love for us in this: That while we were yet sinners, Christ died for us."*

So how can you be saved? You must give over ALL of your trust to God, believe that Jesus is Lord of all, and believe that He raised Christ from the dead, and you will be saved. If you wish to pray right now and ask God into your heart, begin by confessing to God that you are a sinner deserving of Hell, and you repent (ie, turn away) from all of your sins, and then ask Jesus to come into your heart and to save you and to forgive you of all of your sins and you will be saved!

Romans 10:9-10 (KJV) - *"That if you confess with your mouth, 'Jesus is Lord,' and believe in your heart that God raised Him from the dead, you will be saved. For it is with your heart that you believe and are justified, and it is with your mouth that you confess and are saved."*

Now if you've just prayed that prayer, praise God and welcome to the family! Now, as a new believer there are two things you should do right away. 1) Confess your new found faith to at least two other people, 2) find a bible and begin reading it, 3) begin praying to God daily, and 4) find a good, bible believing church in your area and begin attending regularly. Put yourself under their leadership and learn all you can. The change it will bring to your life will be amazing! The love of Christ in your life even more so. The best part yet is the Manna God is yet to provide you now, in the future, and all throughout eternity!

FOR YOU ARE

Blessed

Steven Lake